A LITTLE TREASURY
OF
FAMILIAR PROSE

THE LITTLE TREASURIES

A Little Treasury of Familiar Verse
A Little Treasury of Familiar Prose
A Little Treasury of Religious Verse
A Little Treasury of Love Lyrics

other titles in preparation

A LITTLE TREASURY OF

Familiar
Prose

JOHN BAKER
5 ROYAL OPERA ARCADE
LONDON

©

1964

JOHN BAKER PUBLISHERS LTD
FOR THE RICHARDS PRESS
5 ROYAL OPERA ARCADE
PALL MALL, LONDON
S.W.1

Made and printed in England by
STAPLES PRINTERS LIMITED
at their Rochester, Kent, establishment

COMPILER'S NOTE

'GOOD HEAVENS! For more than forty years I have been speaking prose without knowing it!' When M. Jourdain said this in Molière's play he thought he had satisfactorily resolved the matter; but there is more to it than that—there is prose, and prose. Some of the greatest thoughts of the greatest minds have been expressed in verse, but many more have been in prose; and prose worthy of clothing a great thought is a very different affair from the daily talk of M. Jourdain. 'The other harmony,' Dryden called prose, in a shining phrase, and that is the prose of which a representative choice is gathered here. The prose masters are as many and as diverse as the poets, and here they are: Ralegh, Bacon, Walton, Gibbon, Lamb, Carlyle, Arnold, Stevenson . . . truly a treasury, though little.

K.H.

CONTENTS

Whoever wishes to attain an English style . . . must give his days and nights to the volumes of Addison.

SAMUEL JOHNSON

LET TYRANTS FEAR

My loving people, we have been persuaded by some that are careful of our safety to take heed how we commit ourselves to armed multitudes for fear of treachery. But I assure you, I do not desire to live to distrust my faithful and loving people. Let tyrants fear. I have always so behaved myself that, under God, I have placed my chiefest strength and safeguard in the loyal hearts and good will of my subjects, and therefore I am come amongst you all as you see at this time, not for my recreation and disport, but being resolved in the midst and heat of the battle to live or die amongst you all, to lay down for my God and for my kingdom and for my people, my honour and my blood, even in the dust.

I know I have the body of a weak, feeble woman, but I have the heart and stomach of a king, and a king of England, too, and think foul scorn that Parma or Spain, or any prince of Europe, should dare to invade the borders of my realm; for which, rather than any dishonour should grow by me, I myself will take up arms, I myself will be your general, judge and rewarder of every one of your virtues in the field.

QUEEN ELIZABETH I

O ELOQUENT,
JUST AND MIGHTY DEATH!

IT is . . . Death alone that can suddenly make a man to know himself. He tells the proud and the insolent that they are abjects, and humbles them at the instant; makes them cry, complain, and repent, yea, even to hate their fore-passed happiness. He takes the account of the rich, and proves him a beggar; a naked beggar, which hath interest in nothing but in the gravel that fills his mouth. He holds a glass before the eyes of the most beautiful, and makes them see therein their deformity and rottenness; and they acknowledge it.

O eloquent, just and mighty Death! whom none could advise, thou hast persuaded; what none hath dared, thou hast done; and whom all the world hath flattered, thou only hath cast out of the world and despised; thou hast drawn together all the far-stretched greatness, all the pride, cruelty, and ambition of man, and covered it all over with these two narrow words, *Hic jacit*.

SIR WALTER RALEGH

IF THE HILL WILL NOT
COME TO MAHOMET

BOLDNESS is an ill keeper of promise.
Surely, as there are mountebanks for the
natural body: so are there mountebanks for
the politic body: men that undertake great
cures, and perhaps have been lucky, in two
or three experiments, but want the grounds
of science; and therefore cannot hold out.
Nay, you shall see a Bold Fellow, many
times, do Mahomet's miracle. Mahomet
made the people believe, that he would call
an hill to him; and from the top of it, offer
up his prayers for the observers of his law.
The people assembled: Mahomet called the
hill to come to him again and again; and
when the hill stood still, he was never a
whit abashed, but said, 'If the hill will not
come to Mahomet, Mahomet will go to the
hill.' So these men, when they have pro-
mised great matters, and failed most shame-
fully, (yet if they have the perfection of
Boldness) they will but slight it over, and
make a turn, and no more ado.

FRANCIS BACON

14

BUT NOT FOR LOVE . . .

ROSALIND: . . . The poor world is almost six thousand years old, and in all this time there was not any man died in his own person, *videlicet*, in a love-cause. Troilus had his brains dashed out with a Grecian club; yet he did what he could to die before, and he is one of the patterns of love. Leander, he would have lived many a fair year, though Hero had turned nun, if it had not been for a hot midsummer night; for, good youth, he went but forth to wash him in the Hellespont, and, being taken with the cramp, was drowned; and the foolish coroners of that age found it was 'Hero of Sestos'. But these are all lies: men have died from time to time, and worms have eaten them, but not for love.

WILLIAM SHAKESPEARE

MAN
DELIGHTS NOT ME

GUILDENSTERN: My lord, we were sent for.

HAMLET: I will tell you why; so shall my anticipation prevent your discovery, and your secrecy to the king and queen moult no feather. I have of late—but wherefore I know not—lost all my mirth, forgone all custom of exercises; and indeed it goes so heavily with my disposition that this good frame, the earth, seems to me a sterile promontory; this most excellent canopy, the air, look you, this brave o'erhanging firmament, this majestical roof fretted with golden fire, why, it appears no other thing to me than a foul and pestilent congregation of vapours. What a piece of work is man! How noble in reason, how infinite in faculty! in form, in moving, how express and admirable! in action, how like an angel! in apprehension, how like a god! the beauty of the world! the paragon of animals! And yet, to me, what is this quintessence of dust? Man delights not me; no, nor woman neither, though, by your smiling you seem to say so.

ROSENCRANTZ: My lord, there was no such stuff in my thoughts.

WILLIAM SHAKESPEARE

THE DUST IS SPEECHLESS

IT comes equally to us all, and makes us equal when it comes. The ashes of an oak in the chimney are no epitaph of that oak, to tell me how high or how large that was; it tells me not what flocks it sheltered while it stood, nor what men it hurt when it fell. The dust of great persons' graves is speechless too; it says nothing, it distinguishes nothing. As soon the dust of a wretch whom thou wouldest not, as of a Prince whom thou couldest not look upon, will trouble thine eyes, if the wind blow it thither; and when a whirlwind hath blown the dust of the churchyard into the Church, and the man sweeps out the dust of the Church into the churchyard, who will undertake to sift those dusts again, and pronounce this is the patrician, this the noble flour, and this the yeomanry, this the plebeian bran. So is the death of Jesabel (Jesabel was a Queen) expressed: they shall not say, *This is Jesabel*; not only not wonder what it is, nor pity that it should be, but they shall not say, they shall not know, *This is Jesabel*.

JOHN DONNE

GO ON, AND PROSPER

AND you, most high and mighty Princes of this lower world, who at this intricate and various game of war, vie kingdoms, and win crowns; and by the death of your renowned subjects, gain the lives of your bold-hearted enemies; know there is a *Quo Warranto*, whereto you are to give account of your eye-glorious actions, according to the righteous rules of sacred justice: how warrantable it is to rend imperial crowns from off the sovereign heads of their too-weak possessors; or to snatch sceptres from out the conquered hand of heaven-annointed majesty, and by your vast ambitions still to enlarge your large dominions, with kingdoms ravaged from their natural princes, judge you. O let your brave designs, and well-weighted actions, be as just as ye are glorious; and consider, that all your wars, whose ends are not to defend your own possessions, or to recover your dispossessions, are but princely injuries, which none but heaven can right. But where necessity strikes up her hard alarms, or wronged

19

religion beats her jealous marches, go on, and prosper, and let both swords and stratagems proclaim a victory, whose noised renown may fill the world with your eternal glory.

FRANCIS QUARLES

THE CARE OF HEAVEN

GEORGE HERBERT spent much of his childhood in a sweet content under the eye and care of his prudent mother, and the tuition of a chaplain, or tutor to him and two of his brothers, in her own family,— for she was then a widow,—where he continued till about the age of twelve years; and being at that time well instructed in the rules of grammar, he was not long after commended to the care of Dr Neale, who was then Dean of Westminster; and by him to the care of Mr Ireland, who was then Chief Master of that school; where the beauties of his pretty behaviour and wit shined and became so eminent and lovely in this his innocent age, that he seemed to be marked out for piety, and to become the care of heaven, and of a particular good angel to guard and guide him.

IZAAK WALTON

21

OBLIVION SCATTERETH HER POPPY

But the iniquity of oblivion blindly scattereth her poppy, and deals with the memory of men without distinction to merit of perpetuity. Who can but pity the founder of the pyramids? Herostratus lives that burnt the temple of Diana, he is almost lost that built it; Time hath spared the epitaph of Adrian's horse, confounded that of himself. In vain we compute our felicities by the advantage of our good names, since bad have equal durations; and Thersites is like to live as long as Agamemnon. Who knows whether the best of men be known, or whether there be not more remarkable persons forgot, than any that stand remembered in the known account of Time? Without the favour of the everlasting Register, the first man had been as unknown as the last, and Methuselah's long life had been his only chronicle.

Oblivion is not to be hired; the greater part must be content to be as though they had not been; to be found in the register of

God, not in the record of man. Twenty-seven names make up the first story, and the recorded names ever since contain not one living century. The number of the dead long exceedeth all that shall live. The night of time far surpasseth the day, and who knows when was the Equinox? Every hour adds unto that current arithmetic, which scarce stands one moment. And since death must be the Lucina of life, and even Pagans could doubt whether thus to live were to die; since our longest sun sets at right descensions, and makes but winter arches, and therefore it cannot be long before we lie down in darkness, and have our light in ashes; since the brother of Death daily haunts us with dying Mementoes, and Time that grows old itself bids us hope no long duration, diuturnity is a dream and folly of expectation.

SIR THOMAS BROWNE

TO BE OILED AND TRIMMED, BUT NOT TO BE USED

THE Engine. This word, communicable to all machines or instruments, *use* in this city [London] hath confined to signify that which is used to quench scare-fires therein. One Mr Jones, a merchant (living in Austin Friars) fetched the first form thereof from Nuremberg, and obtained a patent of King James, that none should be made without his approbation. Two were begun but not finished in his lifetime, who died in the great plague, *primo Caroli Primi*; since which time, William Burroughs, city founder, now living in Lothbury, hath so completed this instrument, that his additions amount to a new invention, having made it more secure from breaking, and easy to be cleansed; so that, with the striking out of a wedge, it will cleanse itself, and be fit to work again in four minutes.

Since, the aforesaid party hath made about threescore of these engines for city and country. The cooper, carpenter, smith, founder, brazier and turner contribute their skills to the perfecting of it. Yet may the price thereof be compassed for thirty-five pounds.

It hath gained, because it hath saved, many pounds, and (which is invaluable) many lives of men, in this city. The best, though not the biggest, was lately in the church of St James, Clerkenwell, as hath many times been experimented. . . . Since, a newer at St Bridget's church is a better; and no wonder if the younger out-active those who are more ancient. All wished this engine may be brought forth once a quarter, to be scoured, oiled and trimmed, but not to be used. But if there be an occasion thereof, may it effectually perform that for which it was intended.

THOMAS FULLER

A STYLE LIKELY TO LIVE

For although a poet, soaring in the high region of his fancies, with his garland and singing robes about him, might, without apology, speak more of himself than I mean to do; yet for me sitting here below in the cool element of prose, a mortal thing among many readers of no empyreal conceit, to venture and divulge unusual things of myself, I shall petition to the gentler sort, it may not be envy to me. I must say, therefore, that after I had from my first years, by the ceaseless diligence and care of my father (whom God recompense) been exercised to the tongues, and some sciences, as my age would suffer, by sundry masters and teachers, both at home and at the schools, it was found that whether aught was imposed me by them that had the overlooking, or betaken to of mine own choice, in English, or other tongue, prosing or versing, but chiefly this latter, the style, by certain vital signs it had, was likely to live. But much latlier, in the private academies of Italy, whither I was favoured to resort, perceiving that some trifles which I had in memory, composed at under twenty or thereabout (for the manner is, that everyone must give some proof of his wit and reading there), met with acceptance above what was looked for; and other things, which I had shifted in scarcity of books and conveniences to patch up amongst them, were received with written encomiums, which the Italian is not forward to bestow on men from this side the Alps; I began thus far to assent both to them and divers of my friends here at home, and not less to an inward prompting which now grew daily upon me, that by labour and intent study (which I take to be my portion in this life), joined with the strong propensity of nature, I might perhaps leave something so written to aftertimes, as they should not willingly let it die. . . .

JOHN MILTON

BRIEF AUBREY

T.M. Es꜀., an old acquaintance of mine,
hath assured me that about a quarter of a
year after his first wife's death, as he lay in
bed awake with his grand-child, his wife
opened the closet-door, and came into the
chamber by the bed-side, and looked upon
him and stooped down and kissed him;
her lips were warm, he fancied they would
have been cold. He was about to have
embraced her, but was afraid it might have
done him hurt. When she went from him,
he asked her when he should see her again?
She turned about and smiled, but said
nothing. The closet-door striked as it used
to do, both at her coming in and going out.
He had every night a great coal fire in his
chamber which gave a light as clear almost
as a candle. He was hypochondriacal; he
married two wives since, the latter end of
his life was uneasy.

JOHN AUBREY

A MOST MELODIOUS
TWANG

Anno 1670, not far from Circencester, was an apparition: being demanded whether a good spirit, or a bad? returned no answer, but disappeared with a curious perfume and most melodious twang. Mr W. Lilly believes it was a fairy. So *Propertius*:

Omnia finierat; tenues secessit in auras:
Mansit odor; posses scire fuisse Deam.
Here, her speech ending, fled the beauteus fair,
Melting th' embodied form to thinner air,
Whom the remaining scent a goddess did
   declare.

JOHN AUBREY

THE MOST IMPROPER JUDGE

. . . I have added some original papers of my own [to *Fables*, a volume of translations] which whether they are equal or inferior to my other poems, an author is the most improper judge; and therefore I leave them wholly to the mercy of the reader: I will hope the best, that they will not be condemned; but if they should, I have the excuse of an old gentleman, who mounting on horseback before some ladies, when I was present, got up somewhat heavily, but desired of the fair spectators, that they would count fourscore and eight before they judged him. By the mercy of God, I am already come within twenty years of his number, a cripple in my limbs, but what decays are in my mind, the reader must determine. I think myself as vigorous as ever in the faculties of my soul, excepting only my memory, which is not impaired to any great degree; and if I lose not more of it, I have no great reason to complain. What judgment I had, increases rather than diminishes; and thoughts, such as they are, come crowding in so fast upon me, that my only difficulty is to choose or to reject; to run them into verse, or to give them the other harmony of prose; I have so long studied and practised both, that they are grown into a habit, and become familiar to me. In short, though I may lawfully plead some part of the old gentleman's excuse; yet I will reserve it till I think I have greater need, and ask no grains of allowance for the faults of this my present work, but those which are given of course to human frailty. I will not trouble my reader with the shortness of time in which I writ it; or the several intervals of sickness: they who think too well of their own performances, are apt to boast in their Prefaces how little time their works have cost them; and what other business of more importance interfered; but the reader will be as apt to ask the question, Why they allowed not a longer time to make their works more perfect? and why they had so despicable an opinion of their judges, as to thrust their indigested stuff upon them, as if they deserved no better?

JOHN DRYDEN

MONUMENTS WHICH HAVE
NO POETS

WHEN I am in a serious humour, I very often walk by myself in Westminster Abbey; where the gloominess of the place, and the use to which it is applied, and the condition of the people who lie in it, are apt to fill the mind with a kind of melancholy or rather thoughtfulness, that is not disagreeable. . . .

Upon my going into the church, I entertained myself with the digging of a grave; and saw in every shovelful of it that was thrown up, the fragment of a bone or skull intermixt with a kind of fresh mouldering earth, that some time or other had a place in the composition of a human body. Upon this I began to consider with myself what innumerable multitudes of people lay confused together under the pavement of that ancient cathedral; how men and women, friends and enemies, priests and soldiers, monks and prebendaries, were crumbled amongst one another, and blended together in the same common mass; how beauty, strength, and youth, with old-age, weakness, and deformity, lay undistinguished in the same promiscuous heap of matter.

After having thus surveyed this great magazine of mortality, as it were, in the lump; I examined it more particularly by the accounts which I found on several of the monuments which are raised in every quarter of that ancient fabric. Some of them were covered with such extravagant epitaphs, that, if it were possible for the dead person to be acquainted with them, he would blush at the praises which his friends have bestowed upon him. There are others so excessively modest, that they deliver the character of the person departed in Greek or Hebrew, and by that means are not understood once in a twelvemonth. In the poetical quarter, I found there were poets who had no monuments, and monuments which had no poets. I observed, indeed, that the present war had filled the church with many of these uninhabited monuments, which had been erected to the memory of persons whose bodies were perhaps buried in the plains of Blenheim, or in the bosom of the ocean.

JOSEPH ADDISON

THE MOST DEAD UNCOMFORTABLE TIME

SIR ROGER, after the laudable custom of his ancestors, always keeps open house at Christmas. I learned from him that he had killed eight fat hogs for this season, that he had dealt about his chines very liberally about his neighbours, and that in particular he had sent a string of hog's-puddings with a pack of cards to every poor family in the parish. I have often thought, says Sir Roger, it happens very well that Christmas should fall out in the middle of winter. It is the most dead uncomfortable time of the year, when the poor people would suffer very much from their poverty and cold, if they had not good cheer, warm fires, and Christmas gambols to support them. I love to rejoice their poor hearts at this season, and to see the whole village merry in my great hall. I allow a double quantity of malt to my small beer, and set it a-running for twelve days to every one that calls for it. I have always a piece of cold beef and a mince-pie on the table, and am wonderfully pleased to see my tenants pass away a whole evening in playing their innocent tricks, and smutting one another.

JOSEPH ADDISON

HOW TO BE A EUROPEAN

IT is respectful to bow to the King of England, it is disrespectful to bow to the King of France; it is the rule to curtsy to the Emperor; and the prostration of the whole body is required by Eastern Monarchs. These are established ceremonies, and must be complied with; but why they were established, I defy sense and reason to tell us. It is the same among all ranks, where certain customs are received, and must necessarily be complied with, though by no means the result of sense and reason. As for instance, the very absurd, though almost universal custom of drinking people's healths. Can there be anything in the world less relative to any other man's health, than my drinking a glass of wine? Common sense, certainly, never pointed it out; but yet common sense tells me I must conform to it. Good sense, bids one be civil, and endeavour to please; though nothing but experience and observation can teach one the means, properly adapted to time, place, and persons. This knowledge is the true object of a gentleman's travelling, if he travels as he ought to do. By frequenting good company in every country, he himself becomes of every country; he is no longer an Englishman, a Frenchman, or an Italian; but he is an European: he adopts, respectively, the best manners of every country; and is a Frenchman at Paris, an Italian at Rome, an Englishman at London.

LORD CHESTERFIELD

PURE WITHOUT
SCRUPULOSITY

His prose is the model of the middle style; on grave subjects not formal, on light occasions not grovelling, pure without scrupulosity, and exact without apparent elaboration; always equable, and always easy, without glowing words or pointed sentences. Addison never deviates from his track to snatch a grace; he seeks no ambitious ornaments, and tries no hazardous innovations. His page is always luminous, but never blazes in unexpected splendour.

It was apparently his principle endeavour to avoid all harshness and severity of diction; he is therefore sometimes verbose in his transitions and connections, and sometimes descends too much to the language of conversation; yet, if his language had been less idiomatical, it might have lost somewhat of its genuine anglicism. What he attempted, he performed; he is never feeble, and he did not wish to be energetic; he is never rapid, and he never stagnates. His sentences have neither studied amplitude, nor affected brevity; his periods, though not diligently rounded, are voluble and easy. Whoever wishes to attain an English style, familiar but not coarse, and elegant but not ostentatious, must give his days and nights to the volumes of Addison.

SAMUEL JOHNSON

THE GAIETY OF NATIONS
ECLIPSED

OF Gilbert Walmsley, thus presented to my mind, let me indulge myself in the remembrance. I knew him very early; he was one of the first friends that literature procured me, and I hope that at least my gratitude made me worthy of his notice. He was of an advanced age, and I was only not a boy; yet he never received my notions with contempt. He was a Whig, with all the virulence and malevolence of his party; yet difference of opinion did not keep us apart. I honoured him, and he endured me. He had mingled with the gay world without exemption from its vices and its follies, but had never neglected the cultivation of his mind;

his belief of revelation was unshaken; his
learning preserved his principles; he grew
first regular, and then pious. His studies
had been so various, that I am not able to
name a man of equal knowledge. His
acquaintance with books was great; and
what he did not immediately know, he
could at least tell where to find. Such was
his amplitude of learning, and such his
copiousness of communication, that it may
be doubted whether a day now passes in
which I have not some advantage from his
friendship. At this man's table I enjoyed
many cheerful and instructive hours, with
companions such as are not often found;
with one who has lengthened, and one who
has gladdened life; with Dr James, whose
skill in physic will be long remembered;
and with David Garrick, whom I hoped to
have gratified with this character of our
common friend: But, what are the hopes of
man! I am disappointed, by that stroke of
death which has eclipsed the gaiety of
nations, and impoverished the public stock
of harmless pleasure.

SAMUEL JOHNSON

NOTWITHSTANDING THE
DECLINE OF HIS PERSON

In spring 1775 I was struck with a disorder in my bowels, which at first gave me no alarm, but has since, as I apprehend it, become mortal and incurable. I have suffered very little pain from my disorder; and, what is more strange, have, notwithstanding the great decline of my person, never suffered a moment's abatement of my spirits; insomuch that were I to name a period of my life which I should most choose to pass over again, I might be tempted to point to this later period. I possess the same ardour as ever in study, and the same gaiety in company. I consider, besides, that a man at sixty-five, by dying, cuts off only a few years of infirmities; and though I see many symptoms of my literary reputation's breaking out at last with additional lustre, I know that I could have but very few years to enjoy it. It is difficult to be more detached from life than I am at present.

DAVID HUME

GET INTO THE BOAT,
YOU ROGUE!

[HUME] said . . . that when he was
reading, a few days before, Lucian's
Dialogues of the Dead, among all the excuses
which are alleged to Charon for not entering
readily into his boat, he could not find one
that fitted him: he had no house to finish, he
had no daughter to provide for, he had no
enemies upon whom he wished to revenge
himself. 'I could not well imagine,' said he,
'what excuse I could make to Charon, in
order to obtain a little delay. I have done
everything of consequence that I ever meant
to do, and I could at no time expect to leave
my relations and friends in a better situation
than that in which I am now likely to leave
them: I therefore have all reason to die
contented.' He then diverted himself with
inventing several jocular excuses, which he
supposed he might make to Charon, and
with imagining the very surly answers
which it might suit the character of Charon
to return to them. 'Upon further consideration,' said he, 'I thought I might say to

him, "Good Charon, I have been correcting my works for a new edition. Allow me a little time that I may see how the public receives the alterations." But Charon would answer, "When you have seen the effect of these, you will be for making other alterations. There will be no end to such excuses; so, honest friend, please step into the boat." But I might still urge, "Have a little patience, good Charon, I have been endeavouring to open the eyes of the public. If I live a few years longer, I may have the satisfaction of seeing the downfall of the prevailing systems of superstition." But Charon would then lose all temper and decency. "You loitering rogue, that will not happen these many hundred years. Do you fancy I will grant you a lease for so long a term? Get into the boat this instant, you lazy loitering rogue!" '

ADAM SMITH

THE AGE OF CHIVALRY
IS GONE

It is now sixteen or seventeen years since I saw the Queen of France, then the Dauphiness, at Versailles; and surely never lighted on this orb, which she hardly seemed to touch, a more delightful vision. I saw her just above the horizon, decorating and cheering the elevated sphere she just began to move in; glittering like the morning star, full of life, and splendour, and joy. Oh! what a revolution! and what a heart must I have to contemplate without emotion that elevation and that fall! Little did I dream when she added titles of veneration to those of enthusiastic, distant, respectful love, that she should ever be obliged to carry the sharp antidote against disgrace concealed in that bosom; little did I dream that I should have lived to see such disasters fallen upon her in a nation of gallant men, in a nation of men of honour and of cavaliers. I thought ten thousand swords must have leaped from their scabbards to avenge even a look that threatened her with insult. But the age of Chivalry is gone. That of sophisters, economists, and calculators has succeeded, and the glory of Europe is extinguished for ever. Never, never more, shall we behold that generous loyalty to rank and sex, that proud submission, that dignified obedience, that subordination of the heart, which kept alive, even in servitude itself, the spirit of an exalted freedom. The unbought grace of life, the cheap defence of nations, the nurse of manly sentiments and heroic enterprise is gone! It is gone, that sensibility of principle, that chastity of honour, which felt a stain like a wound, which inspired courage whilst it mitigated ferocity, which ennobled whatever it touched, and under which vice itself lost half its evil, by losing all its grossness.

EDMUND BURKE

A LOFTY STEP IN THE FORUM

My temper is not very susceptible of enthusiasm, and the enthusiasm which I do not feel, I have ever scorned to affect. But at the distance of twenty-five years, I can neither forget nor express the strong emotions which agitated my mind as I first approached and entered the *eternal city*. After a sleepless night, I trod, with a lofty step, the ruins of the Forum; each memorable spot where Romulus *stood*, or Tully spoke, or Caesar fell, was at once present to my eye; and several days of intoxication were lost or enjoyed before I could descend to a cool and minute investigation. . . .

 . . . It was at Rome, on the 15th of October, 1764, as I sat musing amidst the ruins of the Capitol, while the bare-footed friars were singing vespers in the temple of Jupiter, that the idea of writing the decline and fall of the city first started to my mind. . . .

*

I have presumed to mark the moment of conception: I shall now commemorate the hour of my final deliverance. It was on the day, or rather night, of the 27th of June, 1787, that I wrote the last lines of the last page, in a summer-house in my garden. After laying down my pen, I took several turns in a *berceau,* or covered walk of acacias, which commands a prospect of the country, the lake, and the mountains. The air was temperate, the sky was serene, the silver orb of the moon was reflected from the waters, and all nature was silent. I will not dissemble the first emotions of joy on recovery of my freedom, and perhaps, the establishment of my fame. But my pride was soon humbled, and a sober melancholy was spread over my mind, by the idea that I had taken an everlasting leave of an old and agreeable companion, and that whatsoever might be t he future fate of my History, the life of the historian must be short and precarious.

EDWARD GIBBON

AN ISSUE AS GLORIOUS AS THE CAUSE WAS GOOD

EIGHT years have now elapsed since the conclusion of that memorable war which began upon the coast of Portugal, and was brought to its triumphant close before the walls of Toulouse. From the commencement of that contest I entertained the hope and intention of recording its events, being fully persuaded that, if this country should perform its duty as well as the Spaniards and Portugese would discharge theirs, the issue would be as glorious as the cause was good. Having therefore early begun the history, and sedulously pursued it, it would have been easy for me to have brought it forth while the public, in the exultation of success, were eager for its details. But I was not unmindful of what was due to them and to the subject; and I waited patently till, in addition to the means of information which were within my reach, more materials should be supplied by the publications of persons who had been engaged in the war, and till time enough had been allowed for further consideration and fuller knowledge to correct or confirm the views and opinions which I had formed upon the events as they occurred. . . .

*

My task is ended here: and if in the course of this long and faithful history [*History of the Peninsular War*], it should seem that I have anywhere ceased to bear the ways of Providence in mind, or to have admitted a feeling, or given utterance to a thought inconsistent with glory to God in the highest, and good-will towards men, let the benevolent reader impute it to that inadvertence or inaccuracy of expression from which no diligence, however watchful, can always be secure; and as such let him forgive what, if I were conscious of it, I should not easily forgive in myself.

ROBERT SOUTHEY

MEN STARTED, AND
TURNED PALE

THE death of Nelson was felt in England as something more than a public calamity; men started at the intelligence, and turned pale, as if they had heard of the loss of a dear friend. An object of our admiration and affection, of our pride and of our hopes, was suddenly taken from us; and it seemed as if we had never, till then, known how deeply we loved and reverenced him. What the country had lost in its great naval hero — the greatest of our own, and of all former times, was scarcely taken into the account of grief. So perfectly, indeed, had he performed his part, that the maritime war, after the battle of Trafalgar, was considered at an end: the fleets of the enemy were not merely defeated, but destroyed: new navies must be built, and a new race of seamen reared for them, before the possibility of their invading our shores could again be contemplated. It was not, therefore, from any selfish reflection upon the magnitude of our loss that we mourned for him: the general sorrow was of a higher character. The people of England grieved that funeral ceremonies, and public monuments, and posthumous awards, were all which they could now bestow upon him, whom the king, the legislature, and the nation, would have alike delighted to honour; whom every tongue would have blessed; whose presence in every village through which he might have passed would have wakened the church bells, have given schoolboys a holiday, have drawn children from their sports to gaze upon him, and 'old men from the chimney corner', to look upon Nelson ere they died.

ROBERT SOUTHEY

HIS EYE WAS EVER
ON THE SEA

ALL this time sat upon the edge of the deck quite a different character. It was a lad, apparently very poor, very infirm, and very patient. His eye was ever on the sea, with a smile: and if he caught now and then some snatches of these wild legends, it was by accident, and they seemed not to concern him. The waves to him whispered more pleasant stories. He was as one, being with us, but not of us. He heard the bell of dinner ring without stirring; and when some of us pulled out our private stores—our cold meat and our salads—he produced none and seemed to want none. Only a solitary biscuit he had laid in; provision for the one or two days and nights to which these vessels then were oftentimes obliged to prolong their voyage. Upon a nearer acquaintance with him, which he seemed neither to court nor decline, we heard that he was going to Margate with the hope of being admitted into the Infirmary there for sea-bathing. His disease was a scrofula, which appeared to have eaten all over him. He expressed great hopes of a cure; and when we asked him whether he had any friends where he was going, he replied, 'he *had* no friends.'

CHARLES LAMB

CALAMITY MOVES ME

CALAMITY moves me; heroism moves me more. That a nation whose avarice we have so often reprehended, should have cast into the furnace gold and silver, from the insufficiency of brass and iron for arms; that palaces the most magnificent should have been demolished by the proprietor for their beams and rafters in order to build a fleet against us; that the ropes whereby the slaves hauled them down to the new harbour, should in part be composed of hair, for one lock of which kings would have laid down their diadems; that Asdrubal should have found equals, his wife none—my mind, my very limbs, are unsteady with admiration. O Liberty! what art thou to the valiant and brave, when thou art thus to the weak and timid! dearer than life, stronger than death, higher than purest love. Never will I call upon thee where thy name can be profaned, and never shall my soul acknowledge a more exalted Power than thee.

WALTER SAVAGE LANDOR

NO FIELDS OF AMARANTH
THIS SIDE THE GRAVE

AESOP: Breathe, Rhodophè, breathe again
those painless sighs: they belong to thy ver-
nal season. May thy summer of life be calm,
thy autumn calmer, and thy winter never
come.

RODOPHÈ: I must die then earlier.

AESOP: Laodameia died; Helen died;
Leda, the beloved of Jupiter, went before.
It is better to repose in the earth betimes
than to sit up late; better, than to cling
pertinaciously to what we feel crumbling
under us, and to protract an inevitable fall.
We may enjoy the present while we are
insensible of infirmity and decay: but the
present, like a note in music, is nothing but
as it appertains to what is past and what is
to come. There are no fields of amaranth on
this side of the grave: there are no voices,
O Rhodophè, that are not soon mute, however tuneful: there is no name, with whatever
emphasis of passionate love repeated, of
which the echo is not faint at last.

WALTER SAVAGE LANDOR

THE KNOWLEDGE WHICH
THE LEARNED KNOW

Learning is the knowledge of that which is not generally known to others, and which we can only derive at second-hand from books or other artificial sources. The knowledge of that which is before us, or about us, which appeals to our experience, passions, and pursuits, to the bosoms and businesses of men, is not learning. Learning is the knowledge of that which none but the learned know. He is the most learned man who knows the most of what is farthest removed from common life and actual observation, that is of the least practical utility, and least liable to be brought to the test of experience, and that, having been handed down through the greatest number of intermediate stages, is the most full of uncertainty, difficulties, and contradictions. It is seeing with the eyes of others, hearing with their ears, and pinning our faith on their understandings. The learned man prides himself in the knowledge of names and dates, not of men or things. He thinks and cares nothing about his next-door neighbours, but he is deeply read in the tribes and castes of the Hindoos and Calmuc Tartars. He can hardly find his way into the next street, though he is acquainted with the exact dimensions of Constantinople and Pekin. He does not know whether his oldest acquaintance is a knave or a fool, but he can pronounce a pompous lecture on all the principle characters in history. He cannot tell whether an object is black or white, round or square, and yet he is a professed master of the laws of optics and the rules of perspective. He knows as much of what he talks about as a blind man does of colours. He cannot give a satisfactory answer to the plainest question, nor is he ever in the right in any one of his opinions upon any one matter of fact that really comes before him, and yet he gives himself out for an infallible judge on all those points, of which it is impossible that he or any other person living should know anything but by conjecture. He is expert in all the dead and in most of the living languages; but he can neither speak his own fluently, nor write it correctly.

WILLIAM HAZLITT

OSNABRÜCK! OSNABRÜCK!

WHAT we know is, he was journeying
towards Hanover again, hopeful of a little
hunting at the Göhrde, and intending seeing
Osnabrück and his Brother the Bishop there,
as he passed. That day, 21st June 1727,
from some feelings of his own, he was in
great haste for Osnabrück; hurrying along
by extra-post, without real cause save
hurry of mind. He had left his poor old
Maypole of a Mistress on the Dutch
Frontier, that morning, to follow at more
leisure. He was struck by apoplexy on the
road,—arm fallen powerless, early in the
day, head dim and heavy; obviously an
alarming case. But he refused to stop anywhere; refused any surgery but such as
could be done at once. 'Osnabruck!
Osnabruck!' he reiterated, growing visibly
worse. Two subaltern Hanover officials,
Privy-Councillor von Hardenberg, *Kam-
merherr* (Chamberlain) von Fabrice, were
in the carriage with him; King chiefly
dozing, and at last supported in the arms
of Fabrice, was heard murmuring, '*C'est*

fait de moi' ('Tis all over with me)! And 'Osnabrück! Osnabrück!' slumberously reiterated he: 'To Osnabrück, where my poor old Brother, Bishop as they call him, once a little Boy that trotted at my knee with blithe face, will have some human pity on me!' So they rushed along all day, as at the gallop, his few attendants and he; and when the shades of night fell, and speech had now left the poor man, he still passionately gasped some gurgle of a sound like 'Osnabrück';—hanging in the arms of Fabrice, and now evidently in the article of death. What a gallop, sweeping through the slumber of the world: 'To Osnabrück, Osnabrück!'

In the hollow of the night (some say, one in the morning), they reach Osnabrück. And the poor old Brother,—Ernst August, once youngest of six brothers, of seven children, now the one survivor, has human pity in the heart of him full surely. But George is dead; careless of it now. After sixty-seven years of it, he has flung his big burdens,—English crowns, Hanoverian crownlets, sulkinesses, indignations, lean

women and fat, and earthly contradictions
and confusions,—fairly off him; and lies
there.

THOMAS CARLYLE

A KIND OF MILD
ASTONISHMENT

COLERIDGE sat on the brow of Highgate
Hill, in those years, looking down on
London and its smoke-tumult, like a sage
escaped from the inanity of life's battle;
attracting towards him the thoughts of
innumerable brave souls still engaged there.
His express contributions to poetry, philo-
sophy, or any specific province of human
literature and enlightenment, had been
small and sadly intermittent; but he had,
especially among young inquiring men, a
higher than literary, a kind of prophetic or
magician character. . . . Here [in the
garden at Highgate] for hours would
Coleridge talk, concerning all conceivable
or inconceivable things; and liked nothing
better than to have an intelligent, or failing

that, even a silent and patient human listener. He distinguished himself to all that ever heard him as at least the most surprising talker extant in this world,—and to some small minority, by no means to all, as the most excellent.

The good man, he was now getting old, towards sixty perhaps; and gave you the idea of a life that had been full of sufferings; a life heavy-laden, half-vanquished, still swimming painfully in seas of manifold physical and other bewilderment. Brow and head were round, and of massive weight, but the face was flabby and irresolute. The deep eyes, of a light hazel, were as full of sorrow as of inspiration; confused pain looked mildly from them, as in a kind of mild astonishment. The whole figure and air, good and amiable otherwise, might be called flabby and irresolute; expressive of weakness under possibility of strength. He hung loosely on his limbs, with knees bent, and stooping attitude; in walking, he rather shuffled than decisively stept; and a lady once remarked, he never could fix which side of the garden walk would suit him best, but continually shifted, in corkscrew fashion, and kept trying both. A heavy-laden, high-aspiring and surely much suffering man. His voice, naturally soft and good, had contracted itself into a plaintive snuffle and sing-song; he spoke as if preaching,—you would have said, preaching earnestly and also hopelessly the weightiest things. I still recollect his 'object' and 'subject', terms of continual recurrence in the Kantean province; and how he sang and snuffled them into 'om-m-mject' and 'sum-m-mject', with a kind of solemn shake or quaver, as he rolled along.

THOMAS CARLYLE

LIKE A CRAB, BACKWARD

In the origin and perfection of poetry, all
the associations of life were composed of
poetical materials. With us it is decidedly
the reverse. We know too that there are
no Dryads in Hyde-park, nor Naiads in the
Regent's-canal. But barbaric manners and
supernatural interventions are essential to
poetry. Either in the scene, or in the time,
or in both, it must be remote from our
ordinary perceptions. While the historian
and the philosopher are advancing in, and
accellerating the progress of knowledge,
the poet is wallowing in the rubbish of
departed ignorance, and raking up the ashes
of dead savages to find gewgaws and rattles
for the grown babies of the age. Mr Scott
digs up the poachers and cattle-stealers of
the ancient border. Lord Byron cruizes for
thieves and pirates on the shores of the
Morea and among the Greek Islands. Mr
Southey wades through ponderous volumes
of travels and old chronicles, from which
he carefully selects all that is false, useless,
and absurd, as being essentially poetical;

and when he has a commonplace book full
of monstrosities, strings them into an epic.
Mr Wordsworth picks up village legends
from old women and sextons; and Mr
Coleridge, to the valuable information
acquired from similar sources, superadds
the dreams of crazy theologians and the
mysticisms of German metaphysics, and
favours the world with visions in verse, in
which the quadruple elements of sexton,
old woman, Jeremy Taylor, and Emanuel
Kant, are harmonised into a delicious
poetical compound. Mr Moore presents us
with a Persian, and Mr Campbell with a
Pennsylvanian tale, both formed on the
same principle as Mr Southey's epics, by
extracting from a perfunctory and desultory
perusal of a collection of voyages and
travels, all that useful investigation would
not seek for and that common sense would
reject.

*

A poet in our times is a semi-barbarian in a
civilized community. He lives in the days
that are past. His ideas, thoughts, feelings,
associations, are all with barbarous manners,

obsolete customs, and exploded super-
stitions. The march of his intellect is like
that of a crab, backward.

THOMAS LOVE PEACOCK

WHERE THE OWL-WINGED FACULTY DARE NOT SOAR

POETRY is indeed something divine. It is
at once the centre and circumference of
knowledge; it is that which comprehends
all science, and that to which all science must
be referred. It is at the same time the root
and blossom of all other systems of thought;
it is that from which all spring, and that
which adorns all; and that which, if blighted,
denies the fruit and the seed, and withholds
from the barren world the nourishment and
the succession of the scions of the tree of
life. It is the perfect and consummate sur-
face and bloom of all things; it is as the
odour and the colour of the rose to the
texture of the elements which compose it,
as the form and splendour of unfaded beauty
to the secrets of anatomy and corruption.

What were virtue, love, patriotism, friendship,—what were the scenery of this beautiful universe which we inhabit; what were our consolations on this side of the grave—and what were our aspirations beyond it, if poetry did not ascend to bring light and fire from those eternal regions where the owl-winged faculty of calculation dare not ever soar?

*

The most unfailing herald, companion, and follower of the awakening of a great people to work a beneficial change in opinion or institution, is poetry. At such periods there is an accumulation of the power of communicating and receiving intense and impassioned conceptions respecting man and nature. The persons in whom this power resides, may often, as far as regards many portions of their nature, have little apparent correspondence with that spirit of good of which they are the ministers. But even whilst they deny and abjure they are yet compelled to serve, the power which is seated on the throne of their own soul. It is impossible to read the compositions of the most celebrated writers of the present day without being startled with the electric life which burns within their words. They measure the circumference and sound the depths of human nature with a comprehensive and all-penetrating spirit, and they are themselves perhaps the most sincerely astonished at its manifestations; for it is less their spirit than the spirit of the age. Poets are the hierophants of an unapprehended inspiration; the mirrors of the gigantic shadows which futurity casts upon the present; the words which express what they understand not; the trumpets which sing to battle and feel not what they inspire; the influence which is moved not, but moves. Poets are the unacknowledged legislators of the world.

PERCY BYSSHE SHELLEY

BY THE PEOPLE,
FOR THE PEOPLE

FOURSCORE and seven years ago our
fathers brought forth upon this continent a
new nation, conceived in liberty, and dedicated to the proposition that all men are
created equal. Now we are engaged in a
great civil war, testing whether that nation,
or any nation so conceived and so dedicated,
can long endure. We are met on a great
battlefield of that war. We have come to
dedicate a portion of that field as a final
resting place of those who here gave their
lives that that nation might live. It is
altogether fitting and proper that we should
do this. But in a larger sense we cannot
dedicate, we cannot consecrate, we cannot
hallow this ground. The brave men, living
and dead, who struggled here, have con-
secrated it far above our power to add or
detract. The world will little note, nor long
remember, what we say here, but it can
never forget what they did here. It is for
us, the living, rather to be dedicated here
to the unfinished work they have thus far

so nobly advanced. It is rather for us to be here dedicated to the great task remaining before us, that from these honoured dead we take increased devotion to that cause for which they here gave the last full measure of devotion; that we here highly resolve that the dead shall not have died in vain, that this nation, under God, shall have a new birth of freedom; and that government of the people, by the people, and for the people, shall not perish from the earth.

ABRAHAM LINCOLN

THE VALLEY IS GONE,
AND THE GODS WITH IT

You think it a great triumph to make the
sun draw brown landscapes for you! That
was also a discovery and some day may be
useful. But the sun had drawn landscapes
before you, not in brown, but in green, and
blue, and all imaginable colours, here in
England. Not one of you ever looked at
them, then; not one of you cares for the loss
of them, now, when you have shut the sun
out with smoke, so that he can draw nothing
more, except brown blots through a hole in
a box. There was a rocky valley between
Buxton and Bakewell, once upon a time,
divine as the vale of Tempe; you might
have seen the gods there, morning and
evening,—Apollo and all the sweet Muses of
the Light, walking in fair procession on the
lawns of it, and to and fro among the
pinnacles of its crags. You cared neither
for gods nor grass, but for cash (which
you did not know the way to get). You
thought you could get it by what *The Times*
calls 'Railroad Enterprise'. You enter-

prised a railroad through the valley, you blasted its rocks away, heaped thousands of tons of shale into its lovely stream. The valley is gone, and the gods with it; and now, every fool in Buxton can be at Bakewell in half-an-hour; and every fool in Bakewell at Buxton; which you think a lucrative process of exchange, you Fools everywhere!

JOHN RUSKIN

IT WASN'T THE LIFFEY,
BUT . . .

I DRAW back to my own home, twenty years ago, permitted to thank Heaven once more for the peace, and hope, and loveliness of it, and the Elysian walks with Joanie, and Paradisaical with Rosie, under the peach-blossom branches by the little glittering stream which I had paved with crystal for them. I had built behind the highest cluster of laurels a reservoir, from which, on sunny afternoons, I could let a quiet rippling film of water run for a couple of hours down behind the hayfield, where the grass in spring still grew fresh and deep. There used to be always a corncrake or two in it. Twilight after twilight I have hunted that bird, but never once got glimpse of it: the voice was always at the other side of the field, or in the inscrutable air or earth. And the little stream had its falls, and pools, and imaginary lakes. Here and there it laid for itself lines of graceful sand; there and here it lost itself under beads of chalcedony. It wasn't the Liffey, nor the

Nith, nor the Wandel; but the two girls were surely a little cruel to call it 'The Gutter'! Happiest times, for all of us, that ever were to be; not that Joanie and her Arthur are giddy enough, both of them yet, with their five little ones, but they have been sorely anxious about me, and I have been sorrowful enough for myself, since ever I lost sight of that peach-blossom avenue. 'Eden-land' Rosie calls it sometimes in her letters. Whether its tiny river were of the waters of Abana, or Euphrates, or Thamesis, I know not, but they were sweeter to my thirst than the fountains of Trevi or Branda.

JOHN RUSKIN

STEEPED IN SENTIMENT
AS SHE LIES

BEAUTIFUL city! so venerable, so lovely, so unravaged by the fierce intellectual life of our century, so serene!

There are our young barbarians, all at play!

And yet, steeped in sentiment as she lies, spreading her gardens to the moonlight, and whispering from her towers the last enchantments of the Middle Age, who will deny that Oxford, by her ineffable charm, keeps ever calling us nearer to the true goal of all of us, to the ideal, to perfection, — to beauty, in a word, which is only truth seen from another side? — nearer, perhaps, than all the science of Tübingen. Adorable dreamer, whose heart has been so romantic! who hast given thyself so prodigally, given thyself to sides and to heroes not mine, only never to the Philistines! home of lost causes, and forsaken beliefs, and unpopular names, and impossible loyalties! what example could ever so inspire us to keep down the Philistine in ourselves, what teacher could ever so save us from that bondage to which we are all prone, that bondage which Goethe, in his incomparable lines on the death of Schiller, makes it his friend's highest praise (and nobly did Schiller deserve the praise) to have left miles out of sight behind him;—the bondage of '*was uns alle* bändigt, DAS GEMEINE!'[1] She will forgive me, even if I have unwittingly drawn upon her a shot or two aimed at her unworthy son; for she is generous, and the cause in which I fight is, after all, hers. Apparitions of a day, what is our puny warfare against the Philistines compared with the warfare which this queen of romance has been waging against them for centuries, and will wage after we are gone?

MATTHEW ARNOLD

[1] "what Tames us all, THE ORDINARY!"

THE SEDULOUS APE

W<small>HENEVER</small> I read a book or a passage
that particularly pleased me, in which a
thing was said or an effect rendered with
propriety, in which there was either some
conspicuous force or some happy distinction
in the style, I must sit down at once and set
myself to ape that quality. I was unsuccessful, and I knew it; and tried again, and was
again unsuccessful, and was always unsuccessful; but at least in these vain bouts, I
got some practice in rhythm, in harmony,
in construction and the co-ordination of
parts. I have thus played the sedulous ape to
Hazlitt, to Lamb, to Wordsworth, to Sir
Thomas Browne, to Defoe, to Hawthorne,
to Montaigne, to Baudelaire and to Ober-
mann. I remember one of these monkey
tricks, which was called *The Vanity of
Morals*; it was to have had a second part,
The Vanity of Knowledge; and as I had
neither morality nor scholarship, the names
were apt; but the second part was never
attempted, and the first part was written
(which is my reason for recalling it,

ghostlike, from its ashes) no less than three times: first in the manner of Hazlitt, second in the manner of Ruskin, who had cast on me a passing spell, and third, in a laborious pasticcio of Sir Thomas Browne. So with my other works: *Cain*, an epic, was (save the mark!) an imitation of *Sordello*: *Robin Hood*, a tale in verse, took an eclectic middle course among the fields of Keats, Chaucer and Morris: in *Monmouth*, a tragedy, I reclined on the bosom of Mr Swinburne; in my innumerable gouty-footed lyrics I followed many masters; in the first draft of *The King's Pardon*, a tragedy, I was on the trail of no lesser man than John Webster; in the second draft of the same piece, with staggering versatility, I had shifted my allegiance to Congreve. . . .

ROBERT LOUIS STEVENSON

LIST OF SOURCES

79